S·P·Y F·I·L·E·S

TOP SECRET

Illustrated by Teri Gower

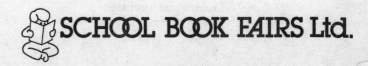

SCHOOL BOOK FAIRS Ltd.

First published in Armada by
William Collins Sons & Co. Ltd in 1988

This School Book Fairs edition
published in 1989

Text copyright © Stephen Thraves 1988
Illustrations copyright © Teri Gower
The Gallery 1988

Printed and bound in Great Britain by
William Collins Sons & Co. Ltd, Glasgow

Ever thought you would make a good spy catcher? Well, here's your chance to prove it! In this unique game book, you have to carry out all the tasks of a real life spy catcher (secret intelligence officer) to try and solve the four espionage cases. Observing sites, tapping phones, shadowing suspects, finding out about them on the Secret Service computer – they're all here! The game can be played either competitively – with you and one or more friends – or solo.

HOW TO PLAY
Competitively

Each of the four cases is contained in a separate spy file, found at the back of the book. Within this file you will find a description of the case, a photograph, surveillance recommendations and access numbers to possibly relevant information held on the Secret Service computer. Having decided which file they wish to tackle, players start by reading the case description. They then take it in turns to carry out a piece of investigation - i.e. choosing one of the numbers in the file and looking up that number in the book. This number can be fron the surveillance recommendation chart, the Secret Service computer chart, or even (in some cases) the photograph - whatever the player wishes. Players can make notes about the information they find for that number but they must keep this information to themselves.

The idea is to keep gathering items of information until one player is able to rule out all suspects except one. If he has sorted out the information correctly, then this suspect should be the spy. The player checks this by making an accusation against him. He announces his choice to the other players and then looks up the appropriate number for that suspect in the accusation list (to be found, upside down, at the back of the spy file). If the book tells him that he has chosen the correct suspect, then the player has won and the game is over. If the book tells him that he is wrong, then he can return to the information-gathering - but he must miss his next five turns before he does so. So, think very carefully before accusing a suspect. For, if you're wrong, not only do you lose these five turns, but you allow your opponents to rule out this particular suspect as well.

HOW TO PLAY
Solo

The solo game is similar to playing competitively, except here you must aim to name the spy in as short a time as possible. Thus, after reading the case description you should note the time. As soon as you have successfully named the spy you should note the time again and the difference between the two represents your score. For every wrong accusation you make, you must add ten minutes to this score. You can find out how good a spy catcher you are by comparing your final score (i.e. the time to complete the game plus any penalty time) with the *ability chart* on the front of the spy file.

Hints on Play

The idea of the game is to be as economical as possible in your investigating. So, first of all, study the photograph for the case very carefully to pick out any clues. For example, if the photograph shows a letter written by the spy (as in *The Invisible Message*), study it to see if there is any unusual spelling. Then look up the *spelling peculiarities* for each suspect to see who doesn't spell like this . . . and therefore can be ruled out from further investigation. Secondly, look out for clues in the surveillance or computer information itself. For example, if when phone-tapped, a suspect says: '*I'm sorry I took so long to answer the phone – I couldn't find my walking stick*', that shows he has a bad leg. If you know from the case file that the spy had fled across a wall, then this person with the bad leg can obviously be eliminated! One final hint – make orderly notes so you can cross refer information and fill in any gaps. For example, during the *trail* of a suspect, the shadow might lose him and not know how long he's been at a certain location. But if you cross refer to the *house observation* on this suspect you will learn what time the suspect returned home. You will therefore roughly be able to work out the information you are missing.

So this is the secret of playing SPY FILES . . . *always look out for clues in the information you receive and use those clues to direct and economize on the rest of your investigating.*

1 A rather bad-tempered, not very popular man. He constantly irritates everyone at the establishment with his chain-smoking but they are all too afraid of him to ask him to cut down. Tends to use his massive weight to bully people into acquiescence.

2 A cigar smoker.

3 No visitors during this time.

4 A very extensive reader and excellent at spelling.

5 Very slim build.

6 CORRECT – on interrogation this person confessed all. The reason for his treacherous activities seemed to be bitterness at constantly being overlooked for promotion.

7

'Hello vicar! This is George Blade speaking. I just wanted to check that Saturday morning is still all right for choir practice.'

8 A rather rash and adventurous young man but vetting didn't find anything suspect about him. Loves most sports – particularly daredevil ones like parachuting and hang-gliding.

9 No phone calls made or received during this time.

10 Quite short-sighted and so always wears glasses. Enjoys going to football matches – usually taking his eight year old son, Jamie.

11 Playing and watching rugby. Seeing women! Photography (especially portraits of pretty females). Regularly dines out and goes to theatre.

12 No phone calls made during this time.

13 Always writes his 'fours' as 4 rather than 4.

14 Rises at 07.45 hrs. Leaves house at 09.30 hrs., driving off in his car. Returns home at 11.15 hrs. and remains at home for rest of day.

15 No phone calls made or received during this time.

16 WRONG – because spy was smoking a filter cigarette. This person only smokes non-filter cigarettes.

17

'Hello, is that the doctor's surgery? This is Michael Vennon here. Could I make an appointment? I sprained my ankle badly a couple of days ago and I can hardly walk on it.'

18 Although in his late 50's, still very fit and active. Dresses very expensively. All his suits and shoes are handmade. Right-handed.

19 WRONG – because this person doesn't use a word containing two R's in any of his phone calls.

20 Gained a distinction in maths at Oxford University. Only problem during his vetting for research lab. post was that he had once been to Moscow as a student – where he fell in love with a Russian girl, Irina. They're not believed to have kept in touch since then, however.

21 Person only away from house between 14.00 and 14.50 hrs. No visitors call during rest of time.

22 No phone calls made or received during this time.

23 Joined naval establishment nearly 20 years ago – although many of those years were spent on attachment to sister naval establishment in USA. Was married with two sons but whole of family tragically wiped out in a car accident. Never driven since.

24 Leaves flat and walks to local supermarket. Returns straight home from supermarket and stays in for rest of day.

25

'Protheroe, this is Gresham here. Just ringing up about that pen of yours. No, I didn't find it in any of my pockets!'

26 Leaves flat at 10.30 hrs. and returns at 11.30 hrs. Leaves flat again at 15.30 hrs. and returns at 18.15 hrs. A female visitor calls at 20.00 hrs. and stays until 23.30 hrs.

27 No phone calls made or received during this time.

28 Graduated in applied mathematics and joined naval establishment after working for a chemicals company. Has been with establishment nearly 15 years now.

29 No phone calls made or received during this time.

30 WRONG – because spy left cigar ash in flat. This person is a non-smoker.

31 Suspect doesn't leave house during this time.

32

'Is that the police station. I wish to complain about my noisy neighbours. They kept me up half of last night!'

33 Analysis of ash in ashtray shows this is from a cigar.

34 Only character flaw is his drinking – but that's quite a serious one! Goes drinking most evenings and several times has drunk so much that he has collapsed. Drink never seems to loosen his tongue, though – and so vetting panel have tended to turn a blind eye to it.

35 No phone calls made or received during this time.

36 Leaves flat and drives towards London. Shadow follows him for about three miles but then loses him at a set of traffic lights.

37

'Wonderful news, Phil – I've won a holiday to Bermuda!'

38 WRONG – because none of this person's visitors uses a word with two L's in the first sentence they speak.

39 A bit of a show-off. Always trying to impress the girls. This worried the vetting panel because they thought he might one day show off about the nature of his work. But he's also a very proud patriot and so they eventually decided he could be trusted.

40 Leaves flat and walks to railway station where he buys computer magazine. Doesn't appear to talk to anyone but does knock into a man in a hat. Returns home and stays in for rest of day.

41 WRONG – because spy's letter was postmarked *London, 24th March*. This person was in Edinburgh from 23rd–25th March.

42 No phone calls made or received during this time.

43 A nervous, quite heavy smoker. Only smokes filter cigarettes.

44

'Hello, old girl! Thanks for the box of cigars. They arrived the day *after* my birthday – but much appreciated all the same!'

45 Photography – although can't take as many pictures as he used to because he has bad arthritis in his fingers. This arthritis has also seriously limited his other main hobby – playing the piano.

46 Person doesn't leave house during this time.

47 Always writes his fours as 4 rather than 4.

48 Works in attic until 14.30 hrs., then sets out in his car. Returns an hour later with a young woman of about twenty. Spends rest of afternoon talking to young woman in sitting room. Woman leaves at 18.00 hrs., subject driving her back to station.

49 5'11" (1.8m) – a little above average.

50 No phone calls made or received during this time.

51 Seems to be a bit of a hypochondriac. Although looks healthy enough, always complaining of pains, indigestion, etc. Irritates his colleagues by continually coughing and sneezing. Has well over average amount of sick leave.

52 Person doesn't leave home during this time.

53 A visitor heard saying: *'Any windows want cleaning, Miss? I'll do the lot for a tenner!'*

54 Person leaves flat at 10.00 hrs. And returns just before midday. Remains at home for rest of day and receives no visitors during this time.

'Hello, Jonathan! It's your father here. I'm sorry about that cigarette burn I caused in your carpet. I insist on buying you a new one.'

56 Average build.

57 No phone calls made or received during this time.

58 Type O.

59 Person returns home at 19.30 hrs. and remains there for rest of evening.

60 Spells words like 'materialize', 'realize' in American fashion – i.e. with an 's' instead of a 'z'.

61 No phone calls made or received during this time.

62 A very big eater, enjoying most foods. Never seems to put on much weight, though, having a very medium build.

63 No phone calls made or received during this time.

64 After graduating in Russian at university, went to Nepal for a year. There he became an experienced mountaineer but had to return to England because the money ran out. Been member of Ministry of Defence special division for 15 years.

65 Subject doesn't leave house during this time.

66

'Hi, Chris! What's this I hear about you doing a parachute jump and breaking your leg?'

67 Receding hairline. Has chipped tooth. Wears contact lenses. Right-handed.

68 No phone calls made or received during this time.

69 Analysis of liquid in glass shows this to be tonic water.

70 A visitor heard saying: *'Hello, Desmond! I was just passing and so I thought I'd see if you knew when the next choir practice was.'*

71 WRONG – because letter says that spy will look out for contact at station on afternoons of 14, 21 and 28 April but this person stays at home all afternoon of 14 April.

72 Loves all types of food, especially fattening things like hamburgers and cream cakes.

73

74 Likes very rich food – although eats in moderation to keep his body in good condition.

75 Subject doesn't leave house during this time.

76 Subject leaves house and walks to nearby bus stop. Shadow stands behind him in queue but when bus comes conductor says there is only room for one more. Subject therefore manages to get away!

77 Short-sighted. Until recently wore contact lenses for this but had eye irritation and so now wears glasses. Rather vain, though, and wears glasses only when absolutely necessary.

78 No phone calls made or received during this time.

79 A rather grumpy person, not very popular with his work colleagues. Never really took to a desk job – although this was forced upon him by his leg injury. Deterioration of leg (now almost completely stiff and cannot walk without aid of stick) has made him more and more irritable with age.

80

'Hello, I'd like to book a table at your restaurant for Saturday evening.'

81 Subject doesn't leave house during this time.

82 Nothing unusual about his spelling.

83 Phone rings during this time but he doesn't answer.

84 A very deceptive person. Appears quite rough and unintelligent but is in fact a brilliant statistician. Once people get to know him, he tends to be very well liked. Loves playing and watching football.

85 WRONG – because spy's jeans size suggests he was of average height. This person is very short. Also, spy had a digital watch. This man refuses to wear a digital watch.

86 No phone calls made or received during this time.

87 Nervously smokes small cigars.

88

'Mother, this is Desmond speaking. Has that cold of yours got any better?'

89 A visitor heard saying: *'Malcolm Heath is the name, antique dealer. I've come to value that painting of yours.'*

90 Subject doesn't leave house during this time.

91 Joined research lab. thirty years ago as a junior clerical officer. Soon worked her way up to senior clerical officer, however, and now virtually seems to run the research lab.! Only Dr Spinks has been there longer than her.

92 Rises at about 08.00 hrs. Receives phone call at about 09.30 hrs. Leaves flat at 13.00 hrs. Returns home at 20.00 hrs. and retires to bed at 23.00 hrs.

93 No phone calls made or received during this time.

94 Graduated in physics from Cambridge University. Has been with naval establishment ever since. Is longest-serving employee there (nearly 38 years).

95

96 Enjoys good wines, champagne.

97 A visitor heard saying: *'Hello, I'm sorry to disturb you but I've come to see if you want any odd jobs doing.'*

98 Subject doesn't leave house during this time..

99 No phone calls made during this time.

100 A rather eccentric man but brilliant inventor. Spends most of his spare time inventing things. Hates to be disturbed while doing this – and so rarely answers the phone or door in evenings.

101 No phone calls made or received during this time.

102 WRONG – because letter says that spy will look out for contact at station on afternoons of 14, 21 and 28 April. This person stays at home all those afternoons.

103 Often seen chewing sweets and gum. Rather surprising given his distinguished position!

104 Athletics – particularly hurdling (used to be an international competitor in this event).

105

'Directory Enquiries? Could you give me the number of a Mrs Matthews in the Bath area?'

106 No visitors during this period.

107 Shadow follows subject as he walks from his house, keeping some 50 metres behind. Following him round corner, however, shadow finds the subject has completely disappeared! He'd obviously guessed he was being tailed.

108 Subject remains in house all morning. Walks out to his car at 13.00 hrs. and returns at about 14.30 hrs. with a female passenger. Entertains female in sitting room until 18.00 hrs. She cooks him a meal and they eat from 19.00 hrs. to 21.00 hrs. Retire to separate bedrooms at about 23.00 hrs.

109 No phone calls made or received during this time.

110 Joined naval establishment 28 years ago as a junior scientist. Has progressed slowly but surely since then. Has an invalid wife to care for. Only child is a son, who recently left home to get married.

111 WRONG – because spy had a bus timetable in his back pocket but this person never travels by bus. Also, spy was of a medium build whereas this person is very slim.

112

'Hello, Michael. It's Geraldine here. Is Patricia there? How's that sprained ankle of yours, by the way?'

113 Type O.

114 WRONG – because spy left cigar ash in flat. This person only smokes a pipe.

115 No phone calls made during this time.

116 No visitors during this time.

117 WRONG – because none of suspect's visitors uses a word with two L's in their first sentence.

118 Always writes date with day before month – e.g. *7th* July rather than July *7th*.

119

'Hello, Peter. Archie here. How about a game of snooker tonight?'

120 Is slightly short-sighted and so has to wear glasses for driving, etc. Hair prematurely grey.

121 No phone calls made or received during this time.

122 Small moustache. Wears a monocle. Only able to walk with help of stick. Nicotine-stained fingers on right hand.

123 Subject leaves house at 08.30 hrs. and goes for an hour long jog. Shadow does his best to keep up with him but eventually has to sit down for a rest.

124 No visitors during this period.

125 Joined research lab. nine years ago as a scientific assistant. Still has this post, although he's possibly in line for promotion soon. Never married.

126 Rises at about 08.00 hrs. Works in attic (looks like some sort of laboratory up there) until 13.00 hrs., then leaves house. Returns at about 13.45 hrs. and remains in for rest of day.

127

SPECTACLES SUPPLIED BY:
M.I. O'PEA (OPTICIAN)

128 Quite slim and fit looking. Has bad dress sense – e.g. often wears brown shoes with a dark blue suit.

129 A visitor heard saying: *'Are you Charles Dodd-Brown? You hunt foxes, don't you? Well, I think it's an absolute disgrace!'*

130 Subject doesn't leave house during this time.

131 CORRECT – now that we know who the mole is, we'll make sure that he only receives phony information in future. That should foil the opposition!

132 Always writes a date with day *before* month – i.e. as *9th* December rather than December *9th*.

133 No phone calls made or received during this time.

134 Subject rises at 08.00 hrs. and takes dog for walk at about 08.30 hrs. Subject returns with dog at about 10.30 hrs. Doesn't leave house again during day.

135

'Professor Wyatt? Hello, this is Mr Hands, the watch mender. You'll be delighted to know that your watch is now ready for collection.'

136 A very sporty, health-conscious person – although has never managed to give up his smoking habit. Not only plays sport but also watches a lot – especially tennis and football. His favourite team is Norwich – the city where he spent his childhood.

137 This is a ticket for a performance of the musical *Phantom of the Opera* on November 10th.

138 WRONG – because spy had a packet of chewing gum in his back pocket. This person hates chewing gum.

139 No phone calls made or received during this time.

140 Very fond of game and fresh salmon. Eats very carefully to make sure he keeps in good trim.

141

'Hector, this is Protheroe here. Did you pick up my pen at the office by any chance?'

142 A visitor heard saying: *'Would you like any gardening jobs done, m'am? Lawn-mowing, weeding, digging – you just name it!'*

143 Subject stays at home during this period.

144 Always writes dates with day before month – e.g. *5th* September rather than September *5th*.

145 Rises at 08.00 hrs. Doesn't leave house until afternoon. Departs at 14.20 hrs. and returns at 18.00 hrs.

146 WRONG – because author of letter writes his fours as 4 whereas this person always writes them as 4.

147 Medium build.

'Hello – this is Denholm Voight speaking, secretary of the photography club. I'm afraid our meeting next Tuesday will have to be cancelled.'

149 A nervous, rather frail person. Vetting panel were rather concerned about this nervous disposition but then they decided that it might not be such a drawback after all. He simply wouldn't have the daring ever to become a double agent!

150 WRONG – because spy dropped a ticket for *The Phantom of the Opera* dated November 10th. This person had tickets to see that musical the day before (Nov. 9th). He would hardly have bought tickets for the very next day as well!

151 No phone calls made during this time.

152 A visitor heard saying: *'Hello Desmond! I don't know whether you remember me but I'm your cousin, Larry!'*

153 Subject doesn't leave house during this period.

154 Subject leaves flat and walks towards local town. Shadow follows him for about half a mile but then is stopped by a policeman who accuses him of acting suspiciously. By the time shadow has explained the situation, subject has disappeared!

155

'Hello, mother. It's John. I hope to be coming up to see you both again next weekend. I've just got to make sure I can get the Friday off.'

156 Long-sighted and always has to wear glasses for reading. Left-handed.

157 Type O.

158 No visitors during this time.

159 Subject walks to local church. A member of Salvation Army stands outside holding a collection box. Subject drops something into box but this something is hidden by his hand. Shadow couldn't be sure whether it was a coin or not.

'Hi, Phil – it's Martin here. I'm afraid I can't make that squash game this afternoon. I've got to meet someone at the station.'

161 Smokes filter cigarettes. More to settle his nerves than for taste.

162 Very similar to Brigadier Reeves in character – condescending and humourless. Takes his work very seriously and has little time for levity. Very competitive by nature.

163 No phone calls made during this time.

164 A visitor heard saying: *'Excuse me, are you Sean's mother? I'm Craig Callaghan's mother and he says that Sean has been bullying him!'*

165 Subject leaves house at 20.30 hrs. and drives his car to local public house. Shadow follows him and notices someone collecting for asthmatics moving amongst customers. Subject appears to give him something – but shadow couldn't be sure what since a darts player blocks his line of vision at that moment.

166 A very good speller.

167

'Mr Robins? This is the bookmakers. We wondered when you were going to clear your debt with us?'

168 Loves all types of travel – train, bus, ship, plane.

169 Doesn't like beer but occasionally drinks spirits. More often drinks mineral or tonic water. Drinks a lot of coffee while at work.

170 WRONG – because spy left a ticket for a musical in the flat. This person doesn't like musicals.

171 Subject and his wife go for a short drive to nearby river. Take dog for walk along river and then return home.

'Is that the hairdresser's? Could I make an appointment for Saturday afternoon?'

173 WRONG – because spy's letter was postmarked *London, 24th* March. This person was in the Lake District from 17th–31st March.

174 No phone calls made or received during this time.

175 5′4″ (1.63m) – very short.

176 Type O.

177 Subject walks to town and shops at supermarket. Catches taxi back.

178 Subject leaves house at 19.30 hrs. and drives to a friend's house about a mile away. He picks up friend and then drives to an Italian restaurant called *Romero's*. Shadow also enters restaurant, taking a discreet table in corner.

179

'This is Margaret Read speaking. I'm interested in your ad. in the local paper.'

180 Subject rises late at 09.30 hrs., leaving flat only ten minutes later. Returns to flat at 11.30 hrs. and stays in for rest of day. Receives no visitors.

181 No phone calls made or received during this time.

182 Although he has had periods of giving it up, still smokes occasionally. Only smokes filter cigarettes, though, because he is worried about the effect on his health.

183 A good looking, spritely man who looks a lot younger than his real age (50). Very relaxed and easy-going in his approach to work. Extremely good at his job, though. Known to have had left-wing sympathies in his youth but these seem to have moderated with age.

'Sorry to disturb you at such a late hour. I wondered if that Malaysian stamp of yours was still for sale?'

185 A bossy, middle-aged woman. Strictly speaking she is only a senior clerical officer but she virtually runs the research lab. Nearly everyone else in the lab. is scared of her. Never married. No close relationship known.

186 Type O.

187 No phone calls made during this time.

188 Subject returns from a fox hunt at about 17.00 hrs. He then drives 15 mile journey back to his home.

189 Subject makes short walk to local church. She drops something into a collection box being held by a woman outside church. Shadow is fairly sure it was only a coin but can't be absolutely positive.

190

'Sorry, I think I must have the wrong number. I wanted the railway station. I'm making a journey this afternoon.'

191 WRONG – because spy's football programme is dated October 11th. This person was at another football ground (Anfield) on that date.

192 No phone calls made or received during this time.

193 This is a brown shoelace – and therefore the person was presumably wearing brown shoes.

194 A visitor heard saying: *'Evening, Roger. Is your wife in? I wondered if she would like to go to the opera next week.'*

'Dr Richards, I wonder if I could have a word with you about my mother? I'm really worried about that cold of hers.'

196 Subject leaves house for local church at 18.00 hrs. Shadow follows him into church and notices him drop something into collection box that is carried round. Shadow is sure that it was only a coin, however.

197 Subject takes dog for two mile walk to country railway station, where he buys it a bag of chocolate drops at little kiosk. Another man with dog comes up to kiosk and two dogs start fighting. Subject angrily gesticulates at other man but shadow not close enough to hear if this is just a pretence.

198 No phone calls made or received during this time.

199 A highly nervous, paranoic person. Defected from Russia as a young man and convinced that they will one day try and kidnap him. Tends to be a bit of a hypochondriac, often taking sick leave. Very prone to road sickness. Refuses to travel by bus, therefore, always catching a train.

200 Subject walks with help of stick to local railway station where he buys a paper at kiosk. Someone bumps into him and he appears to give him a telling off for not looking where he was going. Shadow too far away to hear precise words that passed, however.

201 WRONG – because sticking plaster dropped in flat showed spy had type O blood. This person has type AB blood.

202

'Is that Colin the Conjuror? I would like to book you for my little boy's birthday party next Wednesday.'

203 In words where an 's' or 'z' can be used (e.g. materialize) always uses a 'z'.

204 No phone calls made or received during this time.

205 Analysis of sweet wrapper shows this was for a cough sweet.

206 No phone calls made or received during this time.

208 Smokes cigars very occasionally – but never in the office because he thinks it's unsociable.

209 Subject spends all this period in cricket ground. Sits on his own and never leaves his seat.

210 Subject walks to railway station. Speaks to man at information desk and jots down a few train times. A woman comes up to him and says something. He points up to station clock, suggesting she had been asking the time.

211 Graduated in medicine from Edinburgh University. Trained to be a surgeon but research lab. persuaded him to join them instead. Specializes in thinking up ways of combating germ warfare.

212 No phone calls made or received during this time.

213 Formerly in the navy where he was a lieutenant. Joined establishment five years ago. Never married, although was once engaged.

214

'Hello, Jeremy. I've managed to get tickets for *The Phantom of the Opera* on November 9th. Hope you and your wife can make that evening!'

215 A gentle, placid man. Although has painful arthritis in his fingers, never complains about it. Has good sense of humour. A highly-principled person.

216 Long-sighted and always wears glasses for reading. Right-handed.

217 No phone calls made or received during this time.

218

'Hello, Richard? This is John here. Did I leave my cigarette case in your car by any chance?'

219 Type O.

220 Subject goes for walk to local park. A woman collecting for old people's home stands at entrance to park but subject enters by another gate to avoid her. Avoids her on way out again as well!

221 A visitor heard saying: *'Sorry, I think I called at the wrong door. I was looking for number 31.'*

222 No phone calls made during this period.

223 Obtained a degree in physics from Cambridge University. Later went on to lecture there. Joined research lab. 12 years ago. Vetting panel were rather concerned about fact that he was very left wing as a student but were eventually satisfied that this was a phase he had grown out of.

224

'Hello, Jeffrey – Miriam here. I'll be coming to see you next Saturday afternoon as planned. Can you meet me off the train?'

225 WRONG – because letter-writer spells 'realize' with a 'z'. This person spells the word with an 's'.

226 No phone calls made or received during this time.

227 Type O.

228 Subject drives short distance to church. As he enters church, a teenager approaches with a collection box. Subject rather rudely brushes him aside, however. Shadow follows him into church but, again, he doesn't give any money to two charity collectors there.

229 No phone calls made during this time.

230 Subject leaves house at 09.30 hrs. and enters car with man (presumably husband) and young boy (presumably son). Shadow follows car to local supermarket. As subject enters supermarket boy insists that they give something to charity collector. Subject rather irritably drops something into collection box.

231 No phone calls made during this time.

232 WRONG – because none of this person's visitors uses a word with two L's in their first sentence.

233 Joined research lab. three years ago after obtaining a degree in applied physics. Only sick leave he's ever had was very recently when he broke his leg doing a parachute jump in the Lake District. Spent two weeks (17th–31st March) in hospital up there.

234

Suggests Medium Build

SIZE: 38 121 USA

235 No phone calls made or received during this time.

236 Very good looking, athletic man. Occasionally grows a moustache but rarely lasts long before he shaves it off again. Doesn't like wearing suits in the office – more often a blazer and casual shoes. Right-handed.

237 Subject drives to golf course where has round of golf. As he leaves golf course a man with a collection box comes up to him. Subject drops something in box and is given a paper flag.

238 Very large. Takes size 17½ shirts!

239 Type O.

240 No visitors during this period.

241

'How are you keeping, Merrick, old chap? Just to let you know that the fox hunt is still okay for Sunday.'

242 Wanted to make his career in the army but had to retire early because of a bad leg injury. Transferred to this special department of Ministry of Defence 15 years ago.

243 Subject walks to local public house where meets a girl friend. Shadow also enters public house and notices someone with a collection box approach the two women. Subject drops something into box – but it is hidden by her hand.

244 Doesn't like travelling by air.

245 Subject walks to local newsagent to buy a newspaper. Man with collection box comes up to him but he brushes him aside.

246 No phone calls made during this period.

247 A visitor heard saying: '*Good evening to you. My name's Tom Cartwright. I'm an antique dealer and I wondered if you had anything that might be of interest to me?*'

248 A very old-fashioned person with old-fashioned views. Very fussy about grammar, spelling. Not very popular at research lab. but his experience is difficult to replace.

249

'Hi, Greg – it's Martin here. How about a game of tennis on Saturday morning?'

250 No phone calls made or received during this period.

251 A visitor heard saying: *'Sorry to disturb you but I wondered if you have ever considered double glazing?'*

252 5'10" (1.78m) – about average.

253 Subject goes for a short walk at about 10.30 hrs. but isn't approached by anyone during this period.

254 Medium build.

255 Subject drives with man (husband?) and boy (son?) to a zoo. Shadow follows them around zoo. As they leave, man collecting for preservation of rare animals approaches. Subject drops something into his box.

256

'Hi, Janet! You'll never guess what – I've broken my leg! I did it during a parachute jump in the Lake District four weeks ago. Had to spend two weeks in hospital up there!'

257 Defected from Russia when he was 24. Used to work as a naval scientist there and so the establishment was keen to use this experience. After a thorough investigation, vetting panel were convinced that he wasn't just a 'plant'.

258 No phone calls made or received during this time.

259 Tends to pick and nibble at food. Often suffers from indigestion as a result.

260 A visitor heard saying: *'I'm collecting any old blankets you might have. They're for the old people's home.'*

261 Usual drink is whisky and soda – although occasionally drinks gin and tonic as well.

262 Subject drives to local supermarket with his wife. A woman collecting for the blind stands outside supermarket and subject drops several coins into her box. Shadow couldn't be sure whether he dropped something else in as well.

263

264 WRONG – because spy was very agile (escaped up drainpipe, remember!) but this person has a very stiff leg.

265 Leaves house and walks to local shops. On way back enters the foyer of the railway station to make a phone call at one of the kiosks. He just finishes the phone call when a woman taps him on the shoulder. She appears to ask him for change but shadow too far away to check whether this was just a pretence.

266 Although in his late 50's, still a very fit, healthy man. When in army was an Olympic gymnast, making him very broad in the chest and shoulders. Right-handed.

267 Subject doesn't leave house during this period.

268 Doesn't smoke – and hates others smoking in his presence.

269 Subject drives car to large mansion about five miles away. On gate of mansion is plaque reading *The Orion Club*. Shadow decided it unwise to follow subject in and waits for him outside. Subject emerges again at midnight, immediately driving back home.

270

'Larry, this is Hector here. Will you be at the stamp auction on Saturday?'

271 Subject leaves house with dog at 14.15 hrs. and returns at 16.00 hrs. This is only occasion he leaves house during day.

272 No phone calls made or received during this time.

273 Doesn't like travelling by plane.

274 No phone calls made or received during this time.

275 Tends to eat very quickly. Not very good table manners.

276 WRONG – because this person doesn't use a word containing two R's in any of his phone calls.

277

'Colonel Chase? Hello, this is Wilfred Manning – the tobacconist. I've finally obtained that special pipe tobacco you ordered!'

278 Subject doesn't leave house during this period.

279 No phone calls made during this period.

280 Subject doesn't leave home during this period.

281 A quiet young man who keeps very much to himself at the secret research lab. A brilliant computer operator. Never likes to discuss his personal affairs. Not known to go out much in the evenings or at weekends.

282 Rises at 07.30 hrs. Leaves house at 09.30 hrs. and returns at 11.00 hrs. with a bag of shopping. Stays in house for rest of day. Receives no visitors during this time.

283 No phone calls made or received during this period.

284 An occasional smoker. Only smokes filter cigarettes.

285 Born in Russia, he fled to the West in 1950 when he was 23 years old. Joined naval establishment in 1951 and has been there ever since.

286 WRONG – because football programme in spy's hand is dated *October 11th*. This person was abroad on that day.

287

'Hello, Diane. Bob speaking. I'm afraid I'll have to cancel tomorrow evening.'

288 Despite his age (50) enjoys such active pursuits as swimming and playing tennis. Very fond of the theatre and dining out. Amateur photographer.

289 Subject leaves house at 20.00 hrs. with his wife. Drives to a nearby restaurant. Shadow attempts to enter restaurant himself but waiter tells him it is fully booked. Subject and wife leave restaurant at about 22.30 hrs. with another couple.

290 Worrying about his health!

291 No visitors during this period.

292 Doesn't drink tea or coffee. Usually drinks tonic water or just plain tap water instead. Likes the occasional whisky.

293 A visitor heard saying: *'Paddy, I just had to come round to congratulate you, you lucky thing. I wish I had won a holiday!'*

294 Typically American in character (he spent first 25 years of his life in New York). Extrovert and full of enthusiasm. Has lots of friends and leads a very active social life. Very popular with women but a confirmed bachelor.

295 Phone rings on several occasions during this period but he doesn't answer.

296 Leaves flat at 12.00 hrs. and returns at 14.30 hrs. Leaves flat again at 15.30 hrs. and returns at 18.00 hrs. Three visitors (one male, two female) call at 20.30 hrs. and stay until just after midnight.

'Doctor Neville? This is Felix Hunter speaking. I've got this troublesome cough and I wondered if you could arrange an X-ray for me?'

298 Subject takes dog for walk to country railway station, where he buys it a bag of chocolate drops at little kiosk. Woman comes up to subject and appears to start chatting to him about dog. Shadow couldn't get near enough to hear *exact* words of conversation.

299 No visitors during this period.

300 Only drinks soft drinks like tomato juice and tonic water.

301 Subject walks to hairdresser's. Shadow watches from outside while she has her hair done. As she comes out, she is approached by a man with a collection box but she is in a hurry to catch a bus back home.

302 Doesn't like travelling by plane. Favourite form of travel is by rail.

'Evening, Mansell. Excuse this cough of mine. Anyway, I'm ringing to find out the arrangements for the grouse shoot.'

304 Collecting lead soldiers. Chess and military campaign games. Going to the theatre.

305 WRONG – because this person has nervous habit of always chewing the end of his pencils. Pencil found in flat hadn't been chewed.

306 This is a discarded sticking plaster. Analysis of blood on it shows this to be type O.

307 No phone calls made during this period.

308 Subject walks to local cinema. Followed through foyer but our shadow somehow managed to lose him once inside cinema.

309 Subject walks to local church. Someone collecting for church restoration fund approaches him as he is about to enter. Subject drops something into box.

310 Very fond of cider. Drinks quite a lot of tea but never touches coffee.

311 No phone calls made during this period.

312 Subject leaves house and drives off in car. Shadow follows but becomes trapped in heavy traffic and loses him.

313 Has been an invaluable member of the research lab. for the last 15 years. The lab. once considered sacking him because of his bad gambling habits (which obviously make him prone to financial bribery by enemy agents) but he has modified his habits since then.

314

'Hello, John! It's mother. When are you coming to visit us again? It's four whole weeks since you were last here.'

315 Subject remains in house all morning – receives no visitors. Walks out to his car at 14.45 hrs. and returns in his car at 16.20 hrs. Remains in for rest of day.

316 No phone calls made or received during this period.

317 Has a small moustache. Has never learnt to drive. Short-sighted and wears little round spectacles for long distance viewing.

318 No phone calls made or received during this period.

319 A visitor heard saying: *'I'm sorry to disturb you but I'm looking for Derby Street. Is it near here?'*

320 Smokes small cigars.

321 A visitor heard saying: *'Excuse me, is that your Vauxhall parked outside? The lights have been left on.'*

322

'Hello, Rachel. This is Jonathan speaking. I'm delighted with the present you sent me!'

323 Subject rises at 09.00 hrs. Leaves flat at 09.45 hrs. and returns with three bags of shopping at 11.30 hrs. Remains at home for rest of day but eight guests call between 20.30 hrs. and 21.00 hrs. Last one leaves just after midnight.

324 No phone calls made during this period.

325 Tennis, swimming, collecting old tobacco pipes and sampling rare tobacco.

326 Subject doesn't leave house during this period.

327 Doesn't trust tap water, thinking it full of harmful chemicals. Always drinks bottled spa water or tonic water instead.

328 Subject doesn't leave house during this period.

329 An excellent speller.

330 WRONG – because letter says that spy will look out for contact at station on afternoons of 14, 21 & 28 April. This person remains at home on each of these afternoons.

331 No phone calls made or received during this period.

332 Educated at East Anglia University and joined naval establishment soon after graduating. Has been with establishment 12 years now and is in line for promotion in near future.

333

'Hello, Harry. It's Percy speaking. Sorry about that phone call yesterday. It's this awful indigestion I'm getting . . . it keeps giving me hiccoughs!'

334 WRONG – because position of items on table in flat suggests spy was right-handed. This person was left-handed.

335 Subject leaves house at 21.00 hrs. and drives his car to local public house. Shadow follows him and watches him walk up to an acquaintance at the bar. Subject returns home just before closing time.

336 No phone calls made during this period.

337 No visitors during this period.

338 WRONG – because person doesn't put anything in charity collection box at any time over weekend.

339 Always writes his fours as ┼ rather than 4.

340 Subject leaves his house and drives off in his car. As shadow follows him on to a roundabout, however, subject gives a wrong direction and confuses him. By time shadow has gone round roundabout again to take correct turning, subject has completely disappeared.

341

'Hello, Phil. Tremor here. I thought I might try and get to a football match this weekend if you would like to come.'

342 A very healthy eater, avoiding most junk food.

343 Subject goes out to car and drives to town where he does some shopping. Stops off at railway station on way back and studies 'arrivals' timetable. Someone else comes and stands next to him. Shadow too far away to hear if anything was said.

344 Quite slim and athletic-looking but has severe arthritis in his fingers. Because of this arthritis never wears shoes with laces.

345 Subject goes shopping with his wife. Buys a small bridge table at an antique shop. As he leaves shop, a man with an Oxfam collection box comes up to him. Our shadow watches from other side of road but just at that moment a large lorry comes past, obscuring his vision.

346 Joined special division after short spells in other departments of Ministry of Defence. Has been to Russia twice on holiday – but was perfectly open about this to security people.

347 Always writes 'four' as 4.

348

'Hi, John – it's Tony. Will you be going to the football match on Saturday? It's a really important game for Portsmouth.'

349 A former naval officer, he still has many characteristics of that way of life. Very brisk and punctual. Hates people being late. His hobbies also reflect his naval background – loves sailing and swimming.

350 No phone calls made during this period.

351 A very energetic and enthusiastic type. Very popular with his colleagues. Only time he gets annoyed is when smokers exhale over him. Very fit and athletic – never had a day off work.

352 A visitor heard saying: '*I'm sorry to disturb you, sir, but my car's broken down and I wondered if I could use your phone.*'

353 Enjoys very rich food – particularly French.

354 Subject doesn't leave house during this period.

355 A big drinker – but only spirits. Drinks either whisky and ginger, or gin and tonic.

356 No visitors during this period.

357 Subject catches bus to town where she enters supermarket. Then walks to just outside railway station to wait for a bus. Man behind her in queue starts talking to her. Both have identical shopping bags and it's possible they might have switched but shadow couldn't be sure.

'Hello, is that the tobacconist and sweet shop? This is Dr Wilson, father of Jamie Wilson. Please don't sell him any more chewing gum!'

359 Has a tattoo on his left arm from his days in the navy. Right-handed.

360 A chain-smoker. Always smokes filter cigarettes.

361 A vegetarian, although will eat fish.

362 Subject drives car to house about 15 miles away. Stays in house for about an hour and then drives back home.

363 Smokes a pipe. Doesn't touch any other form of tobacco.

364 No phone calls made during this period.

365 Subject doesn't leave house during this period.

366 Started his career as a newspaper photographer but objected to some of their methods. Joined Ministry of Defence as a photograph analyst but was transferred after four years to this special division. Now third in charge there.

367 No phone calls made during this period.

368 Doing crosswords and playing chess.

369 Subject leaves local church at 13.00 hrs. and buys a joint of meat at butchers. He then returns home, where he stays for rest of afternoon.

370

'Hello, Oliver. Guess who? It's Irina! Guess the good news! I'm working at the Soviet Embassy in London now. We must meet again!'

371 Subject leaves flat and walks to local tennis court where he meets friend. After game, he walks to railway station. Buys magazine at kiosk. Passer-by loses hat and subject picks it up for him. Shadow not sure whether subject discreetly dropped something into hat.

372 Avoids red meat and sugary foods. Hates chewing gum – and won't even allow his son to eat it.

373 Strong, rugged type. Has a thick beard. Slight limp from a mountaineering accident in his youth. Right-handed.

374

'Hello, Geoffrey. I wondered if you and your wife could make dinner some time next week?'

375 Subject drives 15 miles to large house in country. Takes part in fox hunt.

376 No visitors during this period.

377 Despite his eccentricities and vagueness, a very good speller.

378 Subject leaves flat at 13.45 hrs. and returns with bag of shopping just before 15.30 hrs. Doesn't leave flat again during period of observation and receives no visitors.

'Hello, is that Portsmouth football club? Do you have any tickets left for the next Cup match?'

380 A rather surprising person. A brilliant and well-respected scientist but loves watching football and chewing gum! Seems almost schizophrenic. At work always looks smart and distinguished in a suit, but at home dresses in jeans and tatty old sweaters.

381 No phone calls made or received during this period.

382 Smokes small cigars occasionally – but not too often because he worries about the effect on his health.

383 Subject doesn't leave house during this period.

384 No visitors during this period.

'Colonel Chase speaking. I hear you have a collection of old tobacco pipes for sale. I'd like to arrange to come and see them!'

386 Looks a lot younger than his age. Tall, slender with distinguished good looks. Left-handed.

387 No phone calls made during this period.

388 Subject doesn't leave house during this period.

389 A visitor heard saying: *'Protheroe, isn't it? We used to be in the army together. I heard you lived round here, so I thought I'd look you up!'*

390 An American who came over to Britain when he was 25. Worked for an engineering firm and then joined research lab. Has now been at lab. for seven years.

391 Subject only away from house between 14.30 and 15.30 hrs. Only one visitor calls during rest of time – a young woman who kisses him at door and hands him a bag of shopping.

392 No phone calls made or received during this period.

393

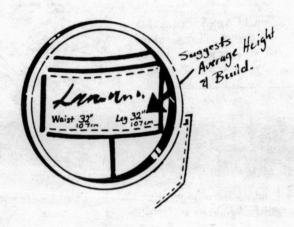

Suggests Average Height & Build.

Waist 32" 107cm   Leg 32" 107cm

394 CORRECT – after eliminating all the other employees, we decided to keep a very close watch on this person's activities. It wasn't long before he was seen with 'The Weasel' again!

395 Tall, slim, sandy-haired. Right-handed. Usually dresses very casually in sports jacket rather than suit when at work.

396 Subject drives to cricket ground. A woman is collecting for medical research outside ground but subject doesn't go near her.

397 No phone calls made during this period.

398 Position of these items to right of document suggests the user was right-handed.

399 Type AB.

400

'Hello, George – I wondered whether you would be at the club on Saturday?'

401 Subject remains home throughout day. Receives a visitor (a middle-aged woman) at 15.00 hrs. She entertains her until 17.00 hrs.

402 Subject leaves flat and walks to local public house. There he meets a couple of friends. Leaves public house via railway station. There he meets an old man with walking stick. Subject takes old man's arm and hails taxi.

403 Wears contact lenses and so doesn't smoke that often because it irritates his eyes. Occasionally can't resist, however.

404 WRONG – because spy's shirt was a size 15½ (about average). This person is of a very large build, wearing size 17½ shirts.

405 No phone calls made or received during this period.

406

'Hello, Derek. Just to confirm that choir practice will be on Saturday morning.'

407 A visitor heard saying: '*Good evening – I've come to collect any unwanted books you might have for the old people's library.*'

408 Educated at Eton, then went to Sandhurst. Officer in army for seven years before joining Ministry of Defence. Been there six years now.

409 No visitors during this period.

410 No phone calls made during this period.

411 Always writes his eights with join at top of figure (i.e. as 8 rather than ୪).

412

'Hello, Gerry. It's Peter here. How about meeting for a jar or two tonight?'

413 CORRECT – unlike all the other employees, there is nothing that can eliminate this person from suspicion. True, the person doesn't go to railway station on either the 21st or 28th April but they do go on the 14 April. If the contact had been met *then*, there would have been no need to go to the station on the next two Saturdays!

414 5'11" (1.8m) – slightly above average.

415 No visitors during this period.

416

'Hello, is that Roger Boyd? This is the university athletics' club. We heard you were once an international athlete and wondered whether you would help with our coaching?'

417 Subject doesn't leave house during this period.

418 Subject walks with help of stick (his right leg is in plaster) to local railway station where he buys a paper at kiosk. Passer-by asks how he broke his leg. Subject drops paper and passer-by picks it up for him. Shadow couldn't be sure whether anything was discreetly handed over at this point.

419 No phone calls made during this period.

420 A rather eccentric man, but brilliant scientist. Tends to have vivid imagination and sees enemy agents in everyone he meets. This makes him very cautious in his behaviour – he takes very roundabout routes whenever he goes anywhere (even if it's a simple walk to the shops!).

'Hello, Rachel. This is Jonathan speaking. I'm delighted with the present you sent me!'

422 Subject leaves house and walks to local bookmakers. Then walks to local railway station, where meets a middle-aged woman off train. He gives her a bunch of flowers and then drives her back to his house. He takes her back to railway station a couple of hours later.

423 5'10" (1.78m) – about average.

424 Analysis of fragments reveals these to be a crushed indigestion tablet.

'Hello, Bob. It's Cathy speaking. How would you like to come round for dinner on Saturday evening?'

426 A visitor heard saying: *'I'm sorry, I seem to have made a silly mistake. I thought Wally Pritchard lived here.'*

427 No phone calls made during this period.

428 Very particular about both his own and other people's spelling. Pet hate is people who spell words like materialize with an 's'.

429 Subject rises at 07.00 hrs. Leaves house at 10.15 hrs., driving off in his car. Returns just before midday and remains at home for rest of day.

430 In spite of working at naval establishment, he hates seafood!

'Hello, William. It's my son's birthday party this Saturday and I can't decide whether to take him to the zoo or a football match. Any suggestions?'

432 Refuses to travel by bus. Will only travel by car for very short distances.

433 Very fond of wine, but only if accompanying food. Doesn't like tea or coffee – usually drinking fruit juice or mineral water instead.

434 No visitors during this period.

435 Smokes small cigars.

436 Subject doesn't leave house during this period.

437 A visitor heard saying: '*My name's Michael Williams – your local Conservative candidate. I hope I can trust on your vote in the election?*'

'Hello, Catherine. It's Boris. I'm afraid I won't be able to see you on Saturday after all because of this train strike. It makes it impossible for me – you know how I never travel by bus!'

439 Subject doesn't leave house during this period.

440 Subject spends all day working in his attic, except for hour between 15.30 hrs. and 16.30 hrs. when drives off in his car.

441 Medium build.

442 Educated at Winchester College, then went on to Sandhurst. Soon rose through officer ranks to become one of youngest brigadiers ever. Joined special division of Ministry of Defence 26 years ago.

'Hello, Gordon. Douglas speaking. I wondered if you would like to join me in a bit of rock climbing this weekend?'

444 Subject drives about 15 miles to large house in country. Stays there for about an hour and then drives back again.

445 No visitors during this period.

446 WRONG – because subject doesn't put anything in charity collection box at any time over weekend.

447 Studied engineering at Cambridge. Joined secret research lab. immediately after receiving his doctorate and has now been there for nearly 25 years. His wife died last year and has one daughter (20 years old) who lives near Guildford.

448 No phone calls made or received during this period.

449 Subject leaves house with dog at 13.30 hrs. and returns at 15.30 hrs. This is only occasion he leaves house during day.

451 Several nervous habits – has a slight twitch and is always nibbling at biscuits or peanuts. Also has irritating habit of chewing the ends of all his pencils. Right-handed.

452 A visitor heard saying: *'Any carpet cleaning required, sir? We do a very professional job!'*

453 No phone calls made during this period.

454 Although a strong, rugged person, very quiet in the office. Loves the outdoor life but also fond of the theatre and dining out.

455

'Hello, it's Susan speaking. My train should be arriving at about four this afternoon. Perhaps you could pick me up?'

456 5′9″ (1.75m) – slightly less than average.

457 Has large appetite. Especially fond of game and beef steaks.

458 Subject doesn't leave house during this period.

459 A visitor heard saying: *'Billy Davies is the name. Want any gardening tools sharpened, sir? My prices are very reasonable!'*

460

'Hello, George. Felix here. I can't make your cocktail party on November 10th, I'm afraid. Alice and I have got tickets for a musical that evening.'

461 Subject doesn't leave house during this period.

462 Subject leaves his house and drives off in car. Shadow follows him but subject somehow manages to lose him in town centre.

463 A visitor heard saying: '*Good evening, sir. Do you want any carpets or upholstery cleaning?*'

464 Subject doesn't leave house during this period.

465

'Is that the bookshop? Do you have a book entitled *The History of Communist Russia*?'

466 Hates to drive and therefore uses public transport a lot.

467 Long-sighted and so always has to wear glasses for reading. Has a slight limp in his left leg.

468 Grouse-shooting. Walking. Tennis. Collecting antique firearms.

469 Subject doesn't leave house during this period.

470

'Hello, Dr Reynolds? Major Tulling speaking. The old leg is really playing me up. Can you prescribe some more painkillers?'

471 Joined the naval establishment straight from university, where he gained a distinction in mathematics. Has now worked there for 15 years – although two of these years were on loan to an American naval establishment.

472 Subject only away from house between 15.00 and 15.45 hrs. No visitors call during rest of period.

473 Always writes dates with day before month – i.e. as *6th* June rather than June *6th*.

474 Subject leaves flat at 09.30 hrs. and returns at 11.30 hrs. Leaves again at 14.30 hrs. and returns at 15.15 hrs. Two visitors call at 18.30 hrs. and stay until early hours of Sunday morning.

'Hello, James. How about another visit to Anfield some time? It was way back on October 11th that we last went to see a match there.'

476 Despite fact that he works in a naval establishment, has a phobia of travelling by sea.

477 Long-sighted and always has to wear glasses for reading. Has little 'goatee' beard.

478 No visitors during this period.

479 Mountaineering – although not quite as daring as he used to be in his youth. Bird-watching. Wildlife photography.

480 Subject makes a five mile drive to nearest town. He parks outside an auction room and enters. Shadow follows him in. Subject makes a bid for some stamps being auctioned but his bid is bettered. Returns home soon after.

'Ronald, I've got the most wonderful news. I've just won a holiday in a newspaper competition!'

482 Joined research lab. just after outbreak of Second World War. Responsible for several brilliant wartime inventions. For last ten years has been second in charge at research lab.

483 Walks to railway station where he meets young woman of about 20 off Guildford train. Kisses her and then drives her back to his house.

484 WRONG – because letter says that spy will look out for contact at station on afternoons of 14, 21 & 28 April but this person stays at home throughout 14 April.

'Dr Popsky? I am – let's say – a friend from your mother country. We've tracked you down, you know. We know where you are!'

486 A quiet, timid but rather eccentric man. Although he has been responsible for many of the modern inventions in use by the navy, in his personal life he is very resistant to new technology. Refuses to use a calculator to add up on – and will only wear a watch with hands!

487 Medium build.

488 Studied languages at university and joined Ministry of Defence as a translator. Moved to special division seven years later and been there over 20 years now.

489 No visitors during this period.

490

'Hello, Geraldine. Bob speaking. Why don't you book theatre tickets for us for next Monday. Not a musical, though – I can't stand them!'

491 Average, fairly athletic build.

492 A rather delicate, quaint man. Tends to be absent-minded, always mislaying his spectacles. Also, a rather nervous person. If he's not anxiously puffing on a cigarette, he's chewing spearmint-flavoured gum.

493 5′10″ (1.78m) – about average.

494 Doesn't like travelling by plane.

495

'Hello, Cecil. This is Phoebe speaking. I've just read an article about a possible cure for arthritis. Shall I send it you?'

496 WRONG – because fact that spy has football programme in his right hand, and watch on his right wrist, suggests he is right-handed. This person is left-handed.

497 A visitor heard saying: '*Look, I really must complain about your dog. It caused me to swerve right across the road!*'

498 A rather fussy eater with a small appetite.

499 A visitor heard saying: '*Hi, my name's Bob Clifton. I'm your new neighbour. I just thought I'd introduce myself.*'

500

'Hello, Cedric, old fellow – I'll see you at the club Saturday evening.'

501 WRONG – because this person doesn't go near anyone collecting for charity over whole of weekend.

502 A very precise speller, never making any mistakes.

503 Subject rises at 08.00 hrs. Leaves house at 14.00 hrs, returning at 15.15 hrs. with two bags of shopping.

504 No phone calls made or received during this period.

505

'Hello, John. I'm sorry I wasn't at the match a couple of weeks ago but I was abroad on business from October 2nd to October 13th.'

506 Loves fish and all types of seafood. Often eats chewing gum but never at work.

507 A visitor heard saying: *'Paddy, I've come to console you, old chap. I hope you're jolly well going to complain to that newspaper!'*

508 Typically Scottish in his attitude to work. Very conscientious and precise. Very kind to his elderly parents. Often takes the Friday off work so he can travel up to Edinburgh to visit them for a long weekend (always catching Thursday night train from Kings Cross).

509 Rises at about 08.15 hrs. Leaves flat at 10.30 hrs. and returns 11.30 hrs. Stays in for rest of day.

510

'Hello, Harry. Percy speaking. I'm ringing to ask you . . . I'm sorry, I'll have to ring you again some other time. I've got hiccoughs!'

511 Eats most food but has a fairly small appetite. His lunch will often consist of just a packet of crisps.

512 Joined department straight from university, where he was considered a brilliant scholar. Expected to rise fast but often overlooked for promotion. Although been there 20 years now, only a couple of rungs higher than when he started.

513 The sea is his favourite form of travel and would much rather travel by ship than plane.

514 Much more of a drinker than an eater. Very fond of pasta, though.

'Sebastian – tomorrow's off, I'm afraid. I'll see you at the hunt on Sunday, though.'

516 Always spells words like 'materialize' with a 'z' rather than an 's'.

517 Leaves flat at 10.00 hrs. and returns at 11.30 hrs. Then stays in until 20.30 hrs., returning home again at 23.30 hrs.

518 WRONG – because letter says that spy will look out for contact at station on afternoons of 14, 21 and 28 April. Although this person does go to station on 14 April, it is in the *morning* not afternoon.

519 An arrogant, humourless man. Although in his late 50's now, still keeps very fit. Very careful in his eating and drinking. Quite a heavy smoker, however (small cigars usually).

'Sorry to disturb you, sir. We're a kitchen design company and we wondered if you would like us to give you an estimate?'

521 A very fussy eater, refusing to try many foods. Tends to eat a lot of chewing gum, because he says it's good for the teeth.

522 5'10" (1.58m) – about average.

523 No visitors during this period.

524

'Ronald, it was all a mistake. I didn't win that holiday after all!'

525 Subject remains in house all day.

526 Subject walks to nearby town, shops at supermarket, then crosses to railway station to stand in taxi queue. A man talks to him in queue but shadow couldn't get near enough to hear what was being said.

527 A very occasional smoker (filter cigarettes only). Always trying to give them up.

528

'Passenger information? Good . . . can you tell me how much the return fare to Brighton is?'

529 WRONG – because this person doesn't use a word containing two R's in any of his phone calls.

530 No visitors during this period.

531 In spite of being quite a sporty person, smokes quite heavily. Only smokes non-filter cigarettes.

532 5′9″ (1.75m) – slightly below average.

533

'Hello, Miriam. I haven't seen you for ages. Why don't you visit me some weekend?'

534 Always writes his fours as ⁴ rather than 4.

535 Subject walks with help of stick to local railway station. Buys a paper at kiosk, asks someone the time (or, at least, pretends to!) and then returns home.

536 Average build.

537

'Hello, is that Mr Hands, the watch mender? I must insist that my watch be ready soon. You've had it now since October 5th – and I simply can't do without it!'

538 Subject drives about two miles to church. Just before entering church, he gives something to a man collecting for medical research.

539 Although is quite a health-conscious person has never managed to give up his smoking. Never smokes at work, though.

540 5'10" (1.78m) – about average.

541 WRONG – because spy had a spectacle case in his back pocket. This person wears contact lenses.

542

'Hi – Edmund speaking. How about meeting for a pint this evening – well, a tonic water in your case!'

543 Only leaves house once, at 15.15 hrs. Returns at 18.00 hrs. and spends rest of evening alone.

544 Occasionally smokes filter cigarettes.

545 No phone calls made or received during this period.

546 WRONG – because spy dropped a shoelace in flat. This person never wears shoes with laces because he has difficulty tying them up.

547 Subject takes dog for walk. Shadow follows them to country railway station where subject is asked way by someone who has just come off train. Person mutters something as he bends down to stroke dog.

548 His only character weakness is his compulsive gambling. After several warnings from the head of the research lab., it is not as bad as it was – but he still can't resist the occasional big bet.

549

550 Subject leaves home in his car but shadow loses him at a set of traffic lights.

551 A teetotaller. Usually drinks pure fruit juices but will occasionally drink tonic water.

552 A charming but rather unscrupulous person. Loves women – and often has two or three girlfriends at a time. Once had a girlfriend from East Germany – which rather worried security people (they thought she might be a spy, planted on him by the Russians).

553 Subject drives to nearby petrol station to fill up his car. As he returns home he is caught up in a traffic jam. A charity collector comes up to his car while he is in the jam but he refuses to open his window for him.

554 No phone calls made during this period.

555 Studied classics at Oxford (where obtained a Blue in athletics). Joined Ministry of Defence immediately afterwards – although given a lot of time off during his early years to train for the Olympics (won a bronze at Munich in 1972).

556 No phone calls made or received during this period.

557 Smokes low-tar cigarettes and, occasionally, small cigars.

558 No phone calls made during this period.

559 Very traditional in his attitude, even though he is only in his early 40's. Quite strict with his young son, Jamie. Doesn't like him to eat too many sweets or junk food.

560 No phone calls made or received during this period.

561 Graduated in marine sciences and later went on to lecture in this subject. Joined naval establishment 12 years ago.

562 No phone calls made or received during this period.

563 No visitors during this period.

564 Type O.

565 Leaves flat and goes for jog. Shadow follows him in his car. Subject leaves flat again several hours later, walking to railway station. There he meets attractive girl off train. He gives her a bunch of flowers and takes her to wine bar before walking her back to station.

566 Occasionally smokes small cigars.

567 Subject leaves flat at 12.00 hrs., returns at 12.45 hrs. Spends rest of afternoon reading magazine and making notes. Someone visits at 19.00 hrs. but only speaks for a few seconds at front door.

568 No phone calls made during this period.

569 Enjoys all types of travel.

570 A bit of a gourmet, often dining out. Doesn't like too much salt in his food. For this reason won't eat salted crisps, etc.

571 Subject goes for walk to local park. Returns home after about half an hour.

572 Eats very carefully and healthily. Tends to eat chewing gum a lot in attempt to cut down on his smoking.

573 Like Brigadier Reeves, educated at Winchester College before going on to Sandhurst Military Academy. It was Brigadier Reeves who suggested him for a job in this special division of the Ministry of Defence. He is now second in charge to him there.

574 Subject drives car to racecourse about ten miles away. As he parks car, a man with collection box comes up to him. Subject takes what appears to be a bank note from his wallet and drops it into box.

575 Analysis of pencil reveals no teeth marks. This is unfortunate because we might have used these to compare with dental records of ten employees.

576 Medium build.

577 No visitors during this period.

THE DARK ROOM

ABILITY CHART

Less than 60 minutes	Immediate Promotion
60-70 minutes	Promotion Recommended
70-80 minutes	Satisfactory
80-90 minutes	Position Under Review!
More than 90 minutes	Demotion!

AGENT'S NOTES ON CASE

Following suspicions that a flat in Mayfair, London, was being rented by an enemy agent, we raided the place yesterday night (Monday). As you can see from the photograph attached, an agent clearly *was* operating there. The flat was full of equipment for taking photographs of secret documents — and converting them into microdots.

Unfortunately, the agent himself escaped just before we broke down the door. He somehow managed to climb up a drainpipe and disappeared across the rooftops. This was obviously a very agile person!

The suddenness of his departure, though, meant that he didn't have time to remove various clues about him in the flat. I have circled objects in the photograph that you might like us to examine more closely — please quote appropriate number.

The secret document photographed by the agent comes from a special division of the Ministry of Defence located near Westminster Abbey. There are only ten people working in this division and so it's almost certain that the agent must be one of these. He presumably took documents from the office safe in the evening, photographed them at the Mayfair flat, and then returned them to the safe the next morning.

The ten employees in question are: Roger Boyd, Major Tulling, Douglas Shearer, Michael Vennon, Brigadier Reeves, Cecil Hammond, Felix Hunter, Capt. Giles, Percy Calthorpe and Colonel Chase. See back of this file for information about these ten people held on our computer.

If any phone taps are required, please use appropriate number below.

RECOMMENDED PHONE TAPS

	ROGER BOYD	MAJOR TULLING	DOUGLAS SHEARER	MICHAEL VENNON	BRIGADIER REEVES	CECIL HAMMOND	FELIX HUNTER	CAPT. GILES	PERCY CALTHORPE	COLONEL CHASE
TUES. EVENING	542	121	192	318	63	35	297	490	206	405
WED. EVENING	57	470	443	17	381	235	460	50	510	78
THUR. EVENING	217	44	274	258	303	495	139	425	333	385
FRI. EVENING	416	68	214	112	556	148	29	287	86	277

EMPLOYEE INFORMATION ON COMPUTER

	ROGER BOYD	MAJOR TULLING	DOUGLAS SHEARER	MICHAEL VENNON	BRIGADIER REEVES	CECIL HAMMOND	FELIX HUNTER	CAPT. GILES	PERCY CALTHORPE	COLONEL CHASE
CHARACTER	351	79	454	183	519	215	149	552	51	162
HISTORY	555	242	64	346	442	366	488	408	512	573
PERSONAL DETAILS	395	122	373	386	18	344	451	236	128	266
HOBBIES	104	304	479	288	468	45	368	11	290	325
SMOKING HABITS	268	2	208	557	320	566	87	435	382	363
EATING HABITS	342	457	361	570	140	511	259	353	275	74
DRINKING HABITS	551	355	169	433	261	310	300	96	327	292
BLOOD TYPE	564	227	113	219	399	176	58	186	239	157

ACCUSATIONS

ROGER BOYD (30), MAJOR TULLING (264), DOUGLAS SHEARER (150),
MICHAEL VENNON (334), BRIGADIER REEVES (201), CECIL HAMMOND (546),
FELIX HUNTER (305), CAPT. GILES (170), PERCY CALTHORPE (6),
COLONEL CHASE (114).

S·P·Y F·I·L·E·S

T·O·P S·E·C·R·E·T

THE FOOTBALL RENDEZVOUS

ABILITY CHART

Less than 50 minutes	Immediate Promotion
50-60 minutes	Promotion Recommended
60-70 minutes	Satisfactory
70-80 minutes	Position Under Review!
More than 80 minutes	Demotion!

AGENT'S NOTES ON CASE

For quite some time now we have known that a foreign agent, "The Weasel", has been receiving information about a secret naval establishment in Portsmouth. What we haven't known, though, is whom he has been receiving his information *from*.

At last, though, we've had a bit of a break. One of our long-range photographers snapped "The Weasel" taking a football programme from a man outside Portsmouth football ground. We're sure the secret information was contained *inside* the football programme.

Unfortunately, the photograph only shows a rear view of the man . . . and he disappeared into the crowd before our photographer could take any further shots. But, if the photograph is enlarged there might well be some clues as to the man's identity. To instruct various areas of enlargement, please refer to appropriate number on photograph.

The type of information the man is passing on means that he must be one of the following ten employees at the secret naval establishment: Dr Wilson, George Wilde, Henry Blessing, Dr Popsky, John Mellows, Saul Maynard, Prof. Wyatt, Boris Nebkoff, Dr Tremor and Prof. Burns.

Computer information held on these ten people can be obtained by referring to grid at back of this file. If, in addition, you would like me to arrange any phone taps on them, please use appropriate code number below.

RECOMMENDED PHONE TAPS

	DR WILSON	GEORGE WILDE	HENRY BLESSING	DR POPSKY	JOHN MELLOWS	SAUL MAYNARD	PROF. WYATT	BORIS NEBKOFF	DR TREMOR	PROF. BURNS
MON. EVENING	431	22	316	109	218	379	537	272	475	174
TUES. EVENING	358	392	55	485	348	520	15	438	341	412
WED. EVENING	93	505	250	283	27	198	135	226	42	560

EMPLOYEE INFORMATION ON COMPUTER

	DR WILSON	GEORGE WILDE	HENRY BLESSING	DR POPSKY	JOHN MELLOWS	SAUL MAYNARD	PROF. WYATT	BORIS NEBKOFF	DR TREMOR	PROF. BURNS
CHARACTER	559	136	492	1	84	349	486	199	380	34
HISTORY	28	332	110	285	471	213	94	257	23	561
HEIGHT	423	49	456	522	414	540	175	532	252	493
BUILD	147	254	536	238	491	56	441	5	487	576
TRAVELLING HABITS	494	168	476	273	569	513	302	432	466	244
SMOKING HABITS	182	539	43	360	531	284	544	161	527	403
EATING HABITS	372	572	498	72	430	506	62	521	103	514
OTHER DETAILS	10	77	156	467	120	359	477	317	216	67

ACCUSATIONS

DR WILSON (138), GEORGE WILDE (286), HENRY BLESSING (496),
DR POPSKY (404), JOHN MELLOWS (16), SAUL MAYNARD (394),
PROF. WYATT (85), BORIS NEBKOFF (111), DR TREMOR (191),
PROF. BURNS (541).

THE INVISIBLE MESSAGE

ABILITY CHART

Less than 50 minutes	Immediate Promotion
50-60 minutes	Promotion Recommended
60-70 minutes	Satisfactory
70-80 minutes	Position Under Review!
More than 80 minutes	Demotion!

AGENT'S NOTES ON CASE

Attached is a photograph of a letter intercepted by one of our agents at the Royal Mail's central sorting office. He became suspicious because of the letter's intended destination — to one of the Iron Curtain countries!

As you can see, there were good grounds for his suspicion. Although the letter looks perfectly innocent on the surface, a secret message was written in between the lines in invisible ink. Chemical treatment by our scientific staff has made this message clearly readable.

The content of the secret message suggests that it could only have been written by one of the personnel working at the Secret Research Laboratory at Newchester (where the Trojan Project is being conducted). These are: Oliver Rice, Dr Todd, Jeffrey Robins, Chris Knight, Dr Spinks, Rachel Thomas, John McDonald, Prof. Hooper, Archie Jones and Martin Green. It is definitely one of these that is our man (or woman)!

Unfortunately, the author of the letter has been very careful not to give much away as to either his handwriting or character. But there are a few clues there — and you might like to refer to information we have on these ten people on our computer (see below for access numbers).

I would also suggest the usual surveillance of these ten people: phone taps, tracking and house observations. If you would like me to organize any of these surveillances, please use appropriate code number (see grid at back of this file).

PERSONNEL INFORMATION ON COMPUTER

	OLIVER RICE	DR TODD	JEFFREY ROBINS	CHRIS KNIGHT	DR SPINKS	RACHEL THOMAS	JOHN McDONALD	PROF. HOOPER	ARCHIE JONES	MARTIN GREEN
CHARACTER	281	100	548	8	248	185	508	420	39	294
HISTORY	20	447	313	233	482	91	211	223	125	390
SPELLING PECULIARITIES	4	203	82	166	428	329	502	377	516	60
HANDWRITING TRAITS	534	347	132	411	47	473	118	13	339	144

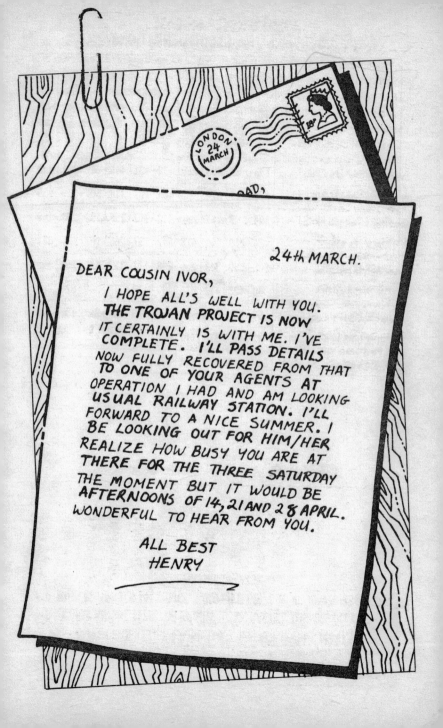

SURVEILLANCE RECOMMENDATIONS

	OLIVER RICE	DR TODD	JEFFREY ROBINS	CHRIS KNIGHT	DR SPINKS	RACHEL THOMAS	JOHN McDONALD	PROF. HOOPER	ARCHIE JONES	MARTIN GREEN
PHONE TAP (14 APRIL)	133	83	533	256	32	421	448	61	331	249
PHONE TAP (21 APRIL)	370	295	224	66	465	101	314	504	119	455
PHONE TAP (28 APRIL)	204	9	167	181	212	322	155	190	263	160
TRACK (14 APRIL)	24	210	461	418	547	357	265	107	36	371
TRACK (21 APRIL)	308	550	343	200	298	177	312	462	154	565
TRACK (28 APRIL)	40	483	422	535	197	439	76	340	526	402
HOUSE OBSERV'N (14 APRIL)	509	126	525	21	134	378	503	282	180	474
HOUSE OBSERV'N (21 APRIL)	92	440	315	472	449	54	543	429	517	26
HOUSE OBSERV'N (28 APRIL)	567	48	108	391	271	401	145	14	323	296

ACCUSATIONS

OLIVER RICE (71), DR TODD (146), JEFFREY ROBINS (484),
CHRIS KNIGHT (173), DR SPINKS (518), RACHEL THOMAS (413),
JOHN McDONALD (41), PROF. HOOPER (102), ARCHIE JONES (330),
MARTIN GREEN (225).

THE MOLE

ABILITY CHART

Less than 45 minutes	Immediate Promotion
45–55 minutes	Promotion Recommended
55–65 minutes	Satisfactory
65–75 minutes	Position Under Review!
More than 75 minutes	Demotion!

AGENT'S NOTES ON CASE

This matter requires your most urgent attention. I have just received a communication from one of our double agents working abroad. It said very little but I suspected that one of the full stops might actually be a microdot. It was!

One glance at the enlarged microdot (see photograph attached) will tell you why our agent felt it so important to use such a device. He obviously wanted to be sure that as few as possible in the department read what he had to say!

As you know, besides myself, there are ten people working in my department. They are: Sir Henry Rawlings, Roger Beasant, Paddy Wilson, Desmond Fraser, George Blade, Charles Dodd-Brown, William Protheroe, Hector Gresham and the two secretaries, Sophie Crane and Margaret Read.

One of these is the "mole" and this is how I propose to identify him/her. Our double agent tells us that he/she uses a word with two R's in the first sentence of the phone call to the contact. Thus, I would suggest a phone tap on all the employees for the next five evenings (to effect this, see grid below) If the employee doesn't use a word with two R's at any time during the week then he/she can be eliminated from our list.

Our double agent also tells us that the contact uses a word with two L's in the first sentence when he visits the mole's home. We therefore plant a bug on the doorstep of each employee and listen to any callers (see grid at back). If none of the employee's callers during the week use a word with two L's, then again he/she can be eliminated.

RECOMMENDED PHONE TAPS

	SIR HENRY RAWLINGS	ROGER BEASANT	PADDY WILSON	DESMOND FRASER	GEORGE BLADE	CHARLES DODD-BROWN	WILLIAM PROTHEROE	HECTOR GRESHAM	SOPHIE CRANE	MARGARET READ
MON. EVENING	558	374	481	88	324	241	141	25	554	105
TUES. EVENING	400	151	37	279	7	562	231	184	172	350
WED. EVENING	12	229	187	336	163	115	364	99	222	246
THUR. EVENING	500	80	524	195	406	367	307	270	410	202
FRI. EVENING	387	545	419	427	453	515	568	397	528	179

I'm afraid to inform you that there is a mole in your department. I'm not sure who it is but I know that he passes information every week. His rather elaborate system is as follows:

First, he rings his contact to let him know when to visit his house. He does this in some sort of code. I'm not sure what the code is but I understand that he uses a word with two Rs in his first sentence to alert his contact that a code is to follow. Second, the contact comes round to his house to let him know when and where he should pass the information. Again, a code is used — the contact uttering a word with two Ls in his first sentence to show that the code is to follow. Third, the mole passes the information at the appointed time and place. This is always at weekends and it is done by pretending to drop money into a charity collection box. In fact, it is his information that he drops into the box... and the charity collector is his messenger.

RECOMMENDED BUGGING AND TRACKING

	SIR HENRY RAWLINGS	ROGER BEASANT	PADDY WILSON	DESMOND FRASER	GEORGE BLADE	CHARLES DODD-BROWN	WILLIAM PROTHEROE	HECTOR GRESHAM	SOPHIE CRANE	MARGARET READ
	1	*2*	*3*	*4*	*5*	*6*	*7*	*8*	*9*	*10*
MON. EVENING BUG	563	106	293	530	260	415	499	291	53	376
TUES. EVENING BUG	97	434	459	311	523	129	389	452	251	164
WED. EVENING BUG	352	319	240	463	70	426	124	221	337	445
THUR. EVENING BUG	116	497	409	152	437	356	3	384	158	142
FRI. EVENING BUG	407	194	507	489	299	89	247	321	478	577
SAT. MORN. TRACK	469	52	262	396	159	444	553	130	464	230
SAT. AFT. TRACK	574	345	388	209	369	46	417	480	301	278
SAT. EVEN. TRACK	269	289	335	59	98	458	178	81	243	328
SUN. MORN. TRACK	571	245	123	362	309	375	538	253	365	153
SUN. AFT. TRACK	237	171	31	220	383	188	267	354	90	255
SUN. EVEN. TRACK	143	436	165	326	196	228	75	280	189	65

ACCUSATIONS

SIR HENRY RAWLINGS (276), ROGER BEASANT (131), PADDY WILSON (529), DESMOND FRASER (501), GEORGE BLADE (19), CHARLES DODD-BROWN (446), WILLIAM PROTHEROE (38), HECTOR GRESHAM (338), SOPHIE CRANE (232), MARGARET READ (117).